VIA DOLOROSA

A Guide for Christians to
Pray the Stations of the Cross

Martin Shannon, CJ

PARACLETE PRESS
BREWSTER, MASSACHUSETTS

2020 First Printing

Via Dolorosa A Guide for Christians to Pray the Stations of the Cross

Copyright © 2020 by Martin Shannon, CJ

ISBN 978-1-64060-464-3

The Paraclete Press name and logo (dove on cross) are trademarks of Paraclete Press, Inc.

Library of Congress Cataloging-in-Publication Data
Names: Shannon, Martin, author.
Title: Via Dolorosa : a guide for Christians to pray the stations of the
    cross / Martin Shannon, CJ.
Description: Brewster, Massachusetts : Paraclete Press, 2020. | Summary: "A
    guide to pray the stations of the cross. At each station, there are
    scripture quotations, along with insightful comments and prayers"–
    Provided by publisher.
Identifiers: LCCN 2019035995 | ISBN 9781640604643 (trade paperback) | ISBN
    9781640604650 (epub) | ISBN 9781640604667 (mobi) | ISBN 9781640604674
    (pdf)
Subjects: LCSH: Stations of the Cross–Meditations. | Benedictine movement
    (Anglican Communion)–Prayers and devotions.
Classification: LCC BX2040 .S53 2020 | DDC 232.96–dc23
LC record available at https://lccn.loc.gov/2019035995

10 9 8 7 6 5 4 3 2 1

Published by Paraclete Press
Brewster, Massachusetts
www.paracletepress.com
Printed in the United States of America

He called the crowd with his disciples
and said to them,
"If any want to become my followers,
let them deny themselves and take up their cross
and follow me."
—Mark 8:34

CONTENTS

INTRODUCTION

Based on early Christian practice, pilgrims to Jerusalem reconstructed the events of Good Friday along the "Way of Suffering," the *Via Dolorosa*. The Spanish nun Egeria writes of her own experience with this in her fourth-century Holy Week journal. In the Middle Ages, the Franciscans and Dominicans particularly picked up on the ritual, and they transported it from Jerusalem to chapels and churches outside the Holy Land. If one could not make the pilgrimage to the place of Jesus's passion, then the "place" could be brought to the pilgrim . . . even in his or her own hometown.

Over the centuries, the stations of the cross spread across Europe and the British Isles. Eventually, fourteen stations were set, with accompanying books of readings and prayers to guide the Good Friday pilgrims as they walked the way with Christ—going "with him" as he bore his cross from the court of Pilate to the hill of Golgotha, from his judgment and condemnation to his death and deposition from the cross.

A Prayer to Begin

O my God, good Jesus,

though I am in every way without merit and unworthy,

grant to me,

who did not deserve to be present at these events in the body,

that I may ponder them faithfully

in my mind

and experience toward you,

my God crucified and put to death for me,

that feeling of compassion

which your innocent Mother and the penitent Magdalene

experienced

at the very hour of your passion.

St. Bonaventure

From *The Tree of Life*

Pilate Condemns Jesus to Die

God did not spare his own Son,
but delivered him up for us all.

Mark 15:1–5, 12–13, 15

As soon as it was morning, the chief priests held a consultation with the elders and scribes and the whole council. They bound Jesus, led him away, and handed him over to Pilate. Pilate asked him, "Are you the King of the Jews?" He answered him, "You say so." Then the chief priests accused him of many things. Pilate asked him again, "Have you no answer? See how many charges they bring against you." But Jesus made no further reply, so that Pilate was amazed.

Pilate spoke to them again, "Then what do you wish me to do with the man you call the King of the Jews?" They shouted back, "Crucify him!"

So Pilate, wishing to satisfy the crowd, released Barabbas for them; and after flogging Jesus, he handed him over to be crucified.

Jesus is condemned to die. The frothing crowd has called for his blood to be spilled . . . and here am I, standing with them. Shouting with them. "Crucify him!" we cry. We're so loud in this courtyard that I keep hearing the echo of the words bouncing off the walls . . . crucify him! . . . crucify him! . . . crucify him! . . .

I know some of these people. A couple of them are my neighbors. I'm pretty sure I even saw my sister. What am I doing here? We're the same people he said he came to save. In the Temple, we say that God has given us the very breath we have to breathe. And here with my friends, I'm using it to yell out, "Crucify him!"

While we scream for his execution, Jesus stands still. Sad. He doesn't say a word. Like a dumb sheep. He seems to be accepting what is about to take place, almost as if he expected it.

Like there was nothing else to be done.

And it looks like Pilate is going to do it.

He's washing his hands.

Good Lord Jesus, I can hardly believe my ears,

and what comes out of my mouth sometimes.

Please do not hold it against me.

You, who hear the song of every sparrow,

hear me as I pray:

We adore you, O Christ, and we praise you;

For by your holy Cross you have redeemed the world.

Jesus Accepts His Cross

The Lord has laid on him the iniquity of us all.

John 19:17

And carrying the cross by himself, [Jesus] went out to what is called The Place of the Skull, which in Hebrew is called Golgotha.

It happened quickly, like they were all prepared.
Once Pilate made up his mind—or we made it up
for him—the cross came out of nowhere. They
set its rough and heavy beam on his shoulders.
It looks like a new one, freshly cut, just for him.
Massive too. It makes his bare back look so small.
After everything he's already been through—
I saw him after the beating they gave him, after
that crown made out of thorns—I don't know
how he can possibly carry it all the way out the
city wall, and up to Golgotha. We'll see.

I've decided to follow, to go the way of the crowd. To watch what happens next. Later they will call this the way of the cross, the way of sorrows. But today I'm just curious. I'm an innocent bystander, really, just going the way everybody else is going.

All that time you knew, Lord
    when you were talking to us about taking
    up our cross—
all that time you knew that yours would be
    taken up first.
When I'm afraid to carry mine,
    the one made just for me,
    help me to remember this day.
Help me to remember my prayer:
    We adore you, O Christ, and we praise you;
    For by your holy Cross you have redeemed the world.

Jesus Falls for the First Time

Surely he has borne our griefs,
and carried our sorrows.

Philippians 2:5–8

Let the same mind be in you that was in
Christ Jesus,
who, though he was in the form of God,
  did not regard equality with God
  as something to be exploited,
but emptied himself,
  taking the form of a slave,
  being born in human likeness.
And being found in human form,
  he humbled himself
  and became obedient to the point of
    death—
even death on a cross.

It was bound to happen. Everybody knew it. The mob was getting bigger and I'd fallen back a ways as people shoved their way into the crowd. So I heard the commotion before I actually saw what was going on. Jesus fell, and from the looks of him, it was not an easy fall. How could it be, with his arms wrapped around that beam? There was nothing to stop him from hitting down hard under the weight. I remember watching him walk and talk through these very streets as if he didn't have a care in the world. That's not quite true. I think he cared very much that we understood what he was talking about, and he seemed a little sad, actually, because I don't think we were getting it.

As he gets up, I can see it looks like he hit his head on a paving stone. That crown they made for him is all askew. When they stand him back up, one of the soldiers rather forcefully sets it straight and jams it down hard to keep it from falling off. It's apparently okay for the man to fall ... but not that crown.

Good Jesus,

> you left everything behind so that you could
> come down to us:
>
> you bent down so you could reach us;
>
> you stooped down to wash our feet;
>
> you bowed your head under the will of your Father.

Down, down you came.

Like water, you kept seeking out the lowest place ...

> my lowest place.

> *We adore you, O Christ, and we praise you;*
>
> *For by your holy Cross you have redeemed the world.*

Jesus Meets His Mother, Mary

A sword will pierce your own soul, also;
and fill your heart with bitter pain.

Luke 2:33–35

And the child's father and mother were amazed at what was being said about him. Then Simeon blessed them and said to his mother Mary, "This child is destined for the falling and the rising of many in Israel, and to be a sign that will be opposed so that the inner thoughts of many will be revealed— and a sword will pierce your own soul too."

I've decided to try to stay closer to Jesus as he goes along. Once I got caught up, I stopped letting people shove me out of the way. Actually, everyone has gotten a little quieter. I think that nasty fall has something to do with it. I doubt he'll be able to keep from doing it again. Even the soldiers seem to be watching him more closely. None of them looks too eager to carry his cross for him.

But someone does push past me, though not roughly at all. Just urgently. Before I know it, she's gone by me and all I can see is the back of her head. It felt almost gentle, the way her hand pressed against my arm, as if she were sorry to move me out of her way. Everybody else, including me, just seems curious and wants to get a closer look at Jesus. But there's something different about the way this woman moves toward him. She seems to be in a hurry.

She pushes past that soldier the same way, and there's nothing he can do about it. Now I see why. Her face is turned ... she's looking at him ... Jesus lifts his head ... and their eyes meet.

I don't know if I want to be here anymore.

On these grimy, dark, and sorrowful streets
> today, dear Jesus,
> how does goodness stay clean?
> how does beauty shine clear?
> how does love make a home?

Blessed is she among women.

Blessed is she who believed.

And blessed is the fruit of her womb.

> *We adore you, O Christ, and we praise you;*
> *For by your holy Cross you have redeemed the world.*

Simon of Cyrene Helps Carry the Cross

*Whoever does not bear his own cross
and come after me,
cannot be my disciple.*

Mark 15:21

They compelled a passer-by, who was coming in from the country, to carry his cross; it was Simon of Cyrene, the father of Alexander and Rufus.

I've decided to stay as close to Jesus as I can, though after what I just witnessed, I wasn't sure I could. Once I saw her face—there's no question it was Jesus's mother—the breath came right out of me . . . those were the first tears I've shed in years. There's a group of women around her now. I see them on the other side, and up ahead a little.

Meantime, we've gone over some pretty rough ground and Jesus has stumbled more than once. I don't know why he doesn't just collapse right in the middle of the street. It's like he actually wants to carry that cross all the way. What for?

There, he just started to go over again. Now everything has stopped. Jesus is just standing there, practically bent in half. Close to him is a man I don't recognize ... one of the pilgrims here for the Passover no doubt. Now I see what's happening. One thing's for sure—that pilgrim has gotten more than he bargained for! Two of the soldiers take the beam off Jesus's shoulders and put it on his. The man's robe is already blood-stained, but he doesn't seem all that upset ... with the blood ... or the cross.

We're moving again.

You talked about the *cross* almost right from
   the beginning, Lord.
It has been one of the harder parts of your
   message for me to get.
I've always liked—but still too seldom believed—
   the part about *love.*
But here ... today ... I know they're the same.
Help me, Jesus, carry both.

   We adore you, O Christ, and we praise you;
   For by your holy Cross you have redeemed the world.

A Woman (Veronica) Wipes the Face of Jesus

Restore us, O Lord God of hosts.
Show the light of your countenance,
and we shall be saved.

Isaiah 53:1–3

Who has believed what we have heard?
And to whom has the arm of the LORD
been revealed?
For he grew up before him like a young plant,
and like a root out of dry ground;
he had no form or majesty that we should
look at him,
nothing in his appearance that we should
desire him.
He was despised and rejected by others;
a man of suffering and acquainted with
infirmity;

and as one from whom others hide their faces
   he was despised, and we held him of no
    account.

In the middle of this ugliness—and there really
isn't any other word to describe what I've seen
in the last few hours—it is amazing to me that
there can be any room for tenderness. When
Jesus saw his mother; when that man (they say he
came all the way from Cyrene) willingly started
to carry Jesus's cross—those were tender
moments. The color of kindness on a black day.
Or like a cool breeze under the burning sun, the
way it skims across your face. It feels so good . . .
and then it's gone before you know it. Could use
one of those today.

Speaking of faces . . . and tenderness . . . back
when we were in the Roman praetorium, there
wasn't a kind face to be found anywhere. Except
maybe Jesus's. Yes, now that I think about it, he
actually did look kind. Even a little peaceful. It sure

wasn't the look on anyone else's face, including mine. Screaming, "Crucify!" at the top of one's lungs doesn't go with a kind expression. But, I see a few more of those in the crowd now. Including this woman who just wiped Jesus's face with a cloth. It must have felt like one of those cool breezes. Face to face.

Kindness meeting kindness.

"Seek my face," you said to the psalmist.
"Your face, Lord, do I seek," he answered.
You must enjoy looking face-to-face, eye-to-eye,
   with us.
Sometimes it's hard to look you in the face.
Or, maybe it's harder for me to be looked at.
Either way, today is not the day to look down.
"Your face, Lord, do I seek."
   We adore you, O Christ, and we praise you;
   For by your holy Cross you have redeemed the world.

Jesus Falls for the Second Time

But as for me, I am a worm and no man,
scorned by all and despised by the people.

Psalm 38:12, 15–17

Those who seek my life lay their snares;
   those who seek to hurt me speak of ruin,
   and meditate treachery all day long.
But it is for you, O Lord, that I wait;
   it is you, O Lord my God, who will answer.
For I pray, "Only do not let them rejoice over me,
   those who boast against me when my foot slips."
For I am ready to fall,
   and my pain is ever with me.

I'd say we are about halfway there, though I've lost sight of
the hill. On any other day you can make this walk in ten
or twelve minutes. But this is not any other day . . . and
this is definitely not any other walk.

It wasn't far from here that Jesus healed that blind man last year. Just around the next corner I think. That was not any other day either. After he bent over and took some dirt at his feet, I remember Jesus stood stock-straight up, tall as a king. He held that bit of dust in his hand like he was about to make the whole world out of it. Then he rubbed some of his own spit into it, and put it on that man's eyes as if he'd done it a million times before. I couldn't believe my own eyes when I saw the man later, seeing me. Some dirt. Some spit. And Jesus of Nazareth. What a difference he made out of that day. It was right about here.

There he goes again. Even without the cross on his back, Jesus is still tripping and stumbling. Falling again. Right into the dirt. This time a string of drool runs down his chin as he gets back up.

I need remaking, Lord. The kind of thing only you
can do.

So, you came. You fell down among us.

Down here with us ... with me ... in the dust
of the ground.

Hold me in your hand when you stand up again.

I need remaking, Lord.

We adore you, O Christ, and we praise you;

For by your holy Cross you have redeemed the world.

Jesus Meets the Women of Jerusalem

*Those who sowed with tears
will reap with songs of joy.*

Luke 23:27–31

A great number of the people followed him, and among them were women who were beating their breasts and wailing for him. But Jesus turned to them and said, "Daughters of Jerusalem, do not weep for me, but weep for yourselves and for your children. For the days are surely coming when they will say, 'Blessed are the barren, and the wombs that never bore, and the breasts that never nursed.' Then they will begin to say to the mountains, 'Fall on us'; and to the hills, 'Cover us.' For if they do this when the wood is green, what will happen when it is dry?"

These streets are rarely quiet and empty, but
today they are unlike anything I've ever seen
before. This parade—at the moment, I really
don't know what else to call it—is more packed
than ever. There's no question that Jesus was
popular when he was teaching and preaching,
and especially when he was giving away food and
healing the sick, but now . . . I think this is the
biggest crowd ever to follow him. Just not for the
same reasons as before. This feels a lot more like
curiosity, mixed with scorn. Morbid, really. Makes
me wonder what I'm still doing here.

That bunch of women stumbling along close
to Jesus looks to be a lot more than curious,
though. And anything but scornful. I've heard
the mourners before, but I've never heard such
weeping as this. It's true. The air is so thick with
misery, it feels like I'm inhaling it. I think they
must be crying for all of us. But Jesus (I don't
know how he has the energy to speak at all) is
telling these women that this isn't the time for

such grief. Save it for when it's really bad, he says.
Really bad? I don't know how anything could ever
be worse than this. Could it?

Sweet Jesus, sometimes tears are all I have.
But sometimes there are none . . .
    and I wish there were.
Most times they're just for me . . .
    and I wish they were for you.
Today, everything should be for you.
Tears . . . dry eyes . . . crying heart . . . dry heart.
    All yours.
    We adore you, O Christ, and we praise you;
    For by your holy Cross you have redeemed the world.

Jesus Falls for the Third Time

He was led like a lamb to the slaughter;
and like a sheep that before its shearers is mute,
so he opened not his mouth.

Isaiah 53:4–6

Surely he has borne our infirmities
    and carried our diseases;
yet we accounted him stricken,
        struck down by God, and afflicted.
But he was wounded for our transgressions,
        crushed for our iniquities;
upon him was the punishment that made us
    whole,
        and by his bruises we are healed.
All we like sheep have gone astray;
        we have all turned to our own way,
        and the Lord has laid on him
        the iniquity of us all.

Jesus just fell again. Third time. Not a moan. Not
a whimper. He landed straight down, with all his
weight on his elbow this time. I don't know how
he didn't break it. You could hear the fall, but
not a sound from him. Silent as a lamb. Just like
he was back with Pilate. We're maybe fifty steps
from the hill now. I don't think he could have
gotten back up without the soldiers manhandling
him, and it looks like they're practically going to
drag him the rest of the way. Third time down has
nearly finished him.

What is it about things happening in threes?
Ever since Noah had three sons it seems like
three is the best number for everything. Abraham
and Sarah had those three visitors at Mamre who
told Sarah about having a son. There were the
three boys that Nebuchadnezzar threw into his
furnace. Can't remember their names, but we're
still singing their song. And Jonah got swallowed
up by that fish—three days and three nights he
spent inside before it threw him up on the beach.

Come to think of it, Jesus said something about three days too. What was that?

Anyway, we're here. I'm so glad to be over with the walking and falling. This is where it ends. Whatever he said about three days, it doesn't matter now.

Lord Jesus, I believe that you are the Word,
    through whom, by whom, for whom
    everything was spoken into being by the Father.
Yet here, today, you are as silent as a void,
    like the day before the first day.
I believe that you are the Beginning, before all
    things,
    and the End, the sum of all things,
    and that in you all things hold together.
Yet here, today, you are the lowest and the last,
    and you cannot even stay on your feet.
What would compel you to be so silent?

Who would compel you to fall so low?

I am silenced and brought down by such mystery.

We adore you, O Christ, and we praise you;

For by your holy Cross you have redeemed the world.

Jesus Is Stripped of His Clothes

They gave me gall to eat;
and when I was thirsty
they gave me vinegar to drink.

Matthew 27:33–35

And when they came to a place called Golgotha (which means Place of a Skull), they offered him wine to drink, mixed with gall; but when he tasted it, he would not drink it. And when they had crucified him, they divided his clothes among themselves by casting lots.

I can't see much over the people standing in front of me. I think Jesus must be lying on the ground now, getting ready to be nailed to the cross. I see the man who had been carrying it, and it's not on his shoulders anymore. Only the bloodstains are there. He looks done in, spent.

There, though. I know what that is. Two of the soldiers are carrying off a couple of small bundles. Those are the clothes Jesus was wearing. His mantle and tunic. That's everything. It is humiliation on top of humiliation. We all know by now that Jesus is going to die, but with no dignity whatsoever? What sort of crime really deserves this kind of punishment? I can't believe his sin could have been that terrible.

Before anything else happens, those soldiers are already playing a game to see who will take the clothes. They can't be worth much. I'm guessing that's not the point. They're laughing while they bet. I think they want Jesus to know how much they're making fun of him. It's not about the clothes. It's about the fun. Jesus is still silent . . . and they're laughing louder than ever.

Humiliation on top of humiliation.

My shame, dear Jesus?

Can I believe that this too was nailed, died,
and buried.

You, who are robed in majesty and girded
with strength;

You, whose train filled the temple;

You, who clothed yourself with only a towel;

You, whose covering was a shroud buried in
a tomb.

Clothe me in a robe of forgiveness;

And cover my shame in a garment of salvation.

We adore you, O Christ, and we praise you;

For by your holy Cross you have redeemed the world.

Jesus Is Nailed to the Cross

They pierce my hands and my feet;
they stare and gloat over me.

Luke 23:33–34

When they came to the place that is called The Skull, they crucified Jesus there with the criminals, one on his right and one on his left. Then Jesus said, "Father, forgive them; for they do not know what they are doing."

You don't have to be able to see to know what is happening now. The sound is piercing. It sends chills down my back. I wish they'd be quicker about it. That one just sounded like a glancing blow on the nail. Not a solid hit. Probably somebody new swinging the hammer. I want it to stop, but I can't stop counting . . . four . . . five . . . six . . .

Some of the people back in Nazareth talked about Jesus when he was a boy, working for his carpenter father in his shop. I'm sure he hurt himself on the tools from time to time. Hit his thumb with a mallet? Cut his finger with a saw? Every carpenter does. There have to be a few people in that town who are sitting at tables or on stools made by Jesus. Or putting their jar of oil on one of his shelves. Or mixing their flour in a bowl made with his young hands. Now the tools of his trade are being used against him. Hands that created are being crushed.

It stopped. Thank God.

"When I look at thy heavens, the work of thy
   fingers ...
   what is man that thou are mindful of him,
   or the son of man that thou dost care for him?"
I, too, am the work of your fingers, Lord, the
   creation of your hands.

But, wood that you once shaped is shaping
   you today.
Hands that once fixed what was broken,
   are fixed to wood and broken by nails.
Who am I that you are mindful of me,
   or that you care for me this much?
   We adore you, O Christ, and we praise you;
   For by your holy Cross you have redeemed the world.

Jesus Dies on the Cross

Christ for us became obedient unto death,
even death on a cross.

Luke 23:44–46

It was now about noon, and darkness came over the whole land until three in the afternoon, while the sun's light failed; and the curtain of the temple was torn in two. Then Jesus, crying with a loud voice, said, "Father, into your hands I commend my spirit." Having said this, he breathed his last.

Even with so much of the crowd still here, what few sounds there are now are clear as a bell toll. A rumble of thunder. A dog barking at night. And a handful of women whose sobs, though subdued, still seem to fill the space around these three crosses. Otherwise, it's deadly still. No one is saying anything.

Jesus has just died.

As long as I live—God willing, for a long time after I live—I will never forget these past three hours. I can almost play out every minute in my mind. From the moment they raised his cross to the moment he dropped his head. It's all right there in front of me, like some kind of moving painting. Even when I look down and close my eyes, I still see him.

But mostly it's the words—his words—that I hear over and over. For that whole agonizing walk from the praetorium to Golgotha, Jesus never made a sound except to those crying women. It was eerie. But once he was hung on that cross, he had some things to say and we all heard him. As if each word was planned ahead. I don't know where he found the breath for it.

And now he's dead.

I'm listening too, Jesus.

Father, forgive them, for they do not know
  what they are doing.
Today you will be with me in paradise.
Woman, behold your son: behold your mother.
My God, my God, why have you forsaken me?
I thirst.
Father, into your hands I commend my spirit.
It is finished.

Please don't let me miss a word you say.
  We adore you, O Christ, and we praise you;
  For by your holy Cross you have redeemed the world.

Jesus Is Taken Down from the Cross

*Her tears run down her cheeks,
and she has none to comfort her.*

John 19:38–40

After these things, Joseph of Arimathea, who was a disciple of Jesus, though a secret one because of his fear of the Jews, asked Pilate to let him take away the body of Jesus. Pilate gave him permission; so he came and removed his body. Nicodemus, who had at first come to Jesus by night, also came, bringing a mixture of myrrh and aloes, weighing about a hundred pounds. They took the body of Jesus and wrapped it with the spices in linen cloths, according to the burial custom of the Jews.

If ever there was an act of gentleness mixed with sorrow, it was what I just witnessed. You might think that a day like this could hold no more sights or sounds to make you catch your breath. And then, another one comes along.

I stayed around after most everyone else had left. Jesus hung there. In an unbelievably cruel act of mercy, the soldiers broke the legs of the men on either side of Jesus. After that, they both died within minutes. The soldiers didn't do the same to Jesus. He was already dead, thank God. But that didn't keep one of them from sticking his spear into him, just to be sure. Then, we just waited.

Out of the corner of my eye, I saw men coming up the hill. I could swear that two of them were both members of the Temple council. They were each carrying something— one had a flowing piece of linen hanging around his shoulders; the other had a large and heavy jar in his hands. When they got to Jesus, they put

down their load and set up a ladder. With help from
a couple of soldiers who removed the nails, and a
young man nearby who jumped in to hold the ladder
(I think he was one of Jesus's close followers), they
ever so carefully let Jesus's body down from the cross.

I'd been so busy watching them that I hadn't seen
the woman sitting below, reaching up to help. The
one who had brushed my arm as she went by in the
crowd. His mother.

The three men gently laid Jesus into her waiting
arms. And for a few moments I watched as she held
him close . . . and rocked him.

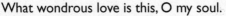

What wondrous love is this, O my soul.
O my soul, what wondrous love is this.[1]
We adore you, O Christ, and we praise you;
For by your holy Cross you have redeemed the world.

1   From an early nineteenth-century American folk hymn, "What
     Wondrous Love Is This."

Jesus Is Placed in the Tomb

*You will not abandon me to the grave,
nor let your holy One see corruption.*

John 19:40–42

Now there was a garden in the place where he was crucified, and in the garden there was a new tomb in which no one had ever been laid. And so, because it was the Jewish day of Preparation, and the tomb was nearby, they laid Jesus there.

After she'd had some private moments holding her dead son—for a few minutes it was as if there was no one there but just the two of them—I watched as the three men, especially the youngest one, tenderly took Jesus's mother by the arms, lifted her up, and drew her off to the side. Then, using that linen shroud one of them had brought, they wrapped up Jesus's body with such care as I have never seen before. Every movement seemed to have purpose, as if they were handling a rare and precious artifact from the beginning of time.

Once he was covered with the linen, the three stood up and looked down at Jesus's wrapped body. They were thinking, I could tell, and whispering among themselves. Then, heaven help me, one of them looked my way. It was the young one. He looked right at me and without a word I knew what he wanted. His eyes said it all. I'll never forget those eyes.

"Come. Help us."

My story must end here, for I still cannot speak nor even think of what I did, and saw, and felt over that next hour, without being there again. Without choking up again. I can only say this. I have never before or since touched anything more dead, nor been touched by anything more alive. I was carrying the body of my Lord . . . but for the life of me, it felt like it was I who was being carried by him.

In life no house, no home
   my Lord on earth might have;
in death no friendly tomb
   but what a stranger gave.
         What may I say?
               Heaven was his home;
               but mine the tomb
   wherein he lay.[2]
   We adore you, O Christ, and we praise you;
   For by your holy Cross you have redeemed the world.

---

2   From Samuel Crossman's seventeenth-century hymn "My Song
Is Love Unknown."

A Prayer For the End

Let every tongue give thanks to you,
Lord our Father,
for the unutterable gift of your most abundant charity.
You have not spared the only Son of your heart,
but you have handed him over
to death
for all of us
that we might have so great and so faithful
an advocate
before your face in heaven.

ST. BONAVENTURE
From *The Tree of Life*

ABOUT PARACLETE PRESS

Who We Are

As the publishing arm of the Community of Jesus, Paraclete Press presents a full expression of Christian belief and practice—from Catholic to Evangelical, from Protestant to Orthodox, reflecting the ecumenical charism of the Community and its dedication to sacred music, the fine arts, and the written word. We publish books, recordings, sheet music, and video/DVDs that nourish the vibrant life of the church and its people.

What We Are Doing

BOOKS | PARACLETE PRESS books show the richness and depth of what it means to be Christian. While Benedictine spirituality is at the heart of who we are and all that we do, our books reflect the Christian experience across many cultures, time periods, and houses of worship.

We have many series, including *Paraclete Essentials*; *Paraclete Fiction*; *Paraclete Poetry*; *Paraclete Giants*; and for children and adults, *All God's Creatures*, books about animals and faith; and *San Damiano Books*, focusing on Franciscan spirituality. Others include *Voices from the Monastery* (men and women monastics writing about living a spiritual life today), *Active Prayer*, and new for young readers: *The Pope's Cat*. We also specialize in gift books for children on the occasions of Baptism and First Communion, as well as other important times in a child's life, and books that bring creativity and liveliness to any adult spiritual life.

THE MOUNT TABOR BOOKS series focuses on the arts and literature as well as liturgical worship and spirituality; it was created in conjunction with the Mount Tabor Ecumenical Centre for Art and Spirituality in Barga, Italy.

MUSIC | THE PARACLETE RECORDINGS label represents the internationally acclaimed choir *Gloriæ Dei Cantores*, the *Gloriæ Dei Cantores Schola*, and the other instrumental artists of the *Arts Empowering Life Foundation*.

Paraclete Press is the exclusive North American distributor for the Gregorian chant recordings from St. Peter's Abbey in Solesmes, France. Paraclete also carries all of the Solesmes chant publications for Mass and the Divine Office, as well as their academic research publications.

In addition, PARACLETE PRESS SHEET MUSIC publishes the work of today's finest composers of sacred choral music, annually reviewing over 1,000 works and releasing between 40 and 60 works for both choir and organ.

VIDEO | Our video/DVDs offer spiritual help, healing, and biblical guidance for a broad range of life issues including grief and loss, marriage, forgiveness, facing death, understanding suicide, bullying, addictions, Alzheimer's, and Christian formation.

Learn more about us at our website
www.paracletepress.com
or phone us toll-free at 1.800.451.5006

SCAN
TO
READ
MORE

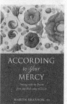